D0579127

Eye Wonder

Arctic and
Antarctic

LONDON, NEW YORK, MUNICH,
MELBOURNE, and DELHI

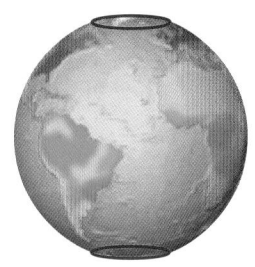

Written and edited by Lorrie Mack
Designed by Laura Roberts-Jensen

Publishing manager Susan Leonard
Picture researchers Laura Roberts-Jensen
and Rob Nunn
Production Seyhan Esen-Yagmurlu
DTP Designer Almudena Díaz
Consultants Bryan and Cherry Alexander

First American Edition, 2006

Published in the United States by
DK Publishing, Inc.
375 Hudson Street
New York, New York 10014

12 13 10 9 8 7 6 5 4
011-ED390-06/06
Copyright © 2006 Dorling Kindersley
Limited, London

ISBN-13 978-0-7566-1980-0

Color reproduction by Colourscan, Singapore
Printed and bound in Italy

Discover more at
www.dk.com

Contents

The ends of the Earth

Earth is shaped like a big ball, or sphere. If you draw a line around its middle, the top half is the northern hemisphere and the bottom half is the southern hemisphere.

On top of the world...

The North Pole sits right at the top of the world. The icy area around it is known as the Arctic. Most of the Arctic is a huge sheet of frozen sea, with pieces of land around the edges.

CANADA

RUSSIAN FEDERATION

ARCTIC OCEAN

ARCTIC

North Pole

GREENLAND

LAPLAND

People

Lots of native peoples have adapted to life in the frozen Arctic. The Antarctic is too cold for humans, though, so only a few scientists call it home.

WINTER

In the middle of Arctic winter (end of December), none of the Sun's rays reach the North Pole, so there is never any daylight—it's always night.

Promised land

Antarctica is a very special place, where science has top priority and the environment is protected. No single country owns it, but lots of powerful ones meet to decide what happens there. This arrangement is called the Antarctic Treaty.

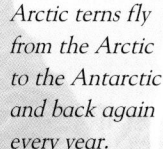

Arctic terns fly from the Arctic to the Antarctic and back again every year.

Antarctic oceans are covered with ice for most of the year.

SOUTHERN OCEAN

Weddell Sea

Antarctic Peninsula

ANTARCTICA

South Pole

LESSER ANTARCTICA

GREATER ANTARCTIC

Ross Ice Shelf

SOUTHERN OCEAN

...and down under

The South Pole is at the opposite end of the Earth, in Antarctica. Made of frozen land covered with ice and surrounded by (mostly) frozen sea, it has the driest, windiest, and coldest climate on Earth.

These penguins live in big groups called colonies.

SUMMER

At the same time, it's summer in the Antarctic, so the Sun never sets and daylight lasts for 24 hours. Arctic summer and Antarctic winter are at the end of June.

Animals

Like people, most animals find the Antarctic too cold to live in. But penguins like it there—they have a thick layer of feathers to keep them warm.

Ice scapes

Polar worlds are like complex and beautiful sculptures made of ice, snow, water, and a little land. They tend to change from one year or season to the next.

Moving ice

Glaciers are thick deposits of ice and snow that move slowly under their own weight. They are formed from freshwater—unlike seawater, this has no salt in it.

Jagged icebergs in the frozen sea look like a city skyline.

When sea ice breaks up, wind and tides push the pieces together to make pressure ridges.

Frost flowers

When the temperature drops in Arctic and Antarctic seas, salt-covered crystals can form on the surface of new ice. These make shapes known as frost or ice flowers.

White caps

Over 90 percent of Antarctica is covered with permanent ice like this—some of it is 13,000 feet (over 4,000 meters) thick! At the other pole, most of Greenland is covered with a single solid ice cap.

Icy facts

- Antarctica's thick covering of ice makes it the highest continent in the world.

- Under the ice shelves around Antarctica, the seas have never been explored.

- Northern oceans that are permanently covered with ice are called the marine Arctic.

Pancake ice

When it gets cold, crystals form on the sea surface, then stick together to form tiny ice floes. These knock into each other, rounding the edges so they look like pancakes.

Frozen sea ice

During the winter, the ice on the frozen sea gradually increases until it is over six feet (two meters) thick in some places—strong enough to land a jet plane on!

FALL

...the sea freezes into ice sheets...

WINTER

...bears hunt on frozen ice...

Ice takes lots of different forms when it melts and freezes again.

SUMMER

...summer ice floes drift...

SPRING

...melting ice forms shallow pools...

Ice floes

In the summer, when the sea is at its warmest (which isn't very warm really), pieces of sea ice called floes tend to drift around in the open water.

Meltwater

When spring comes, sheets of sea ice begin to melt. Sometimes, they get broken up by stormy waves into small, jagged pieces.

Breaking the ice

Special icebreakers are used to move through polar ice, because ordinary ships would get stuck. This one is breaking up the frozen Arctic sea.

A blaze of red against frosty white and blue, this Russian icebreaker is called the Yamal.

Tip of the iceberg

Whether they're near the Arctic or the Antarctic, chunks of ice that break off ice caps or glaciers crash into the sea and become icebergs. Each one bobs around until it finds a balanced position, then floats with the current.

Iceberg facts

• When a new iceberg breaks away, the process is known as *calving*.

• Because they come from glaciers, icebergs are made of freshwater ice.

• Tiny icebergs 3-16 ft (1-5 m) tall are called *bergy bits*.

The biggest part of an iceberg stays hidden under the surface.

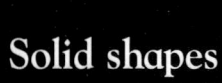

Solid shapes

Icebergs don't look clear because the ice caps and glaciers they come from were formed out of packed snow. Some icebergs have layers of "dirty" ice, picked up by the original glacier when it moved.

Islands of ice

Ice is not as heavy as water, so icebergs float—only a small tip of each one sticks up out of the sea. The biggest berg ever recorded was 90 miles (145 km) wide!

Sea sculptures

Powerful waves crashing into the side of an iceberg form fantastical shapes and shadows. This berg is floating off the northwest coast of Greenland.

KILLER ICE

On its first voyage in 1912, a huge ocean liner called the *Titanic* ran into an iceberg off Newfoundland, Canada. In the middle of the night, the jagged underwater ice ripped huge holes in the ship's side, and within three hours, the *Titanic* had sunk, taking nearly 1,500 people with it.

C	F
50	120
40	100
30	80
20	60
10	40
0	20
10	0
20	
30	20
40	40

— Average Arctic summer 50°F (10°C)

— Fresh water freezes 32°F (0°C)

0 — Sea water freezes 0 °F (-18°C)

— Home freezer -11.2°F (-24°C)

20 — Average Antarctic summer -22 °F (-30°C)

40 — Average Arctic winter -40 °F (-40°C)

Out in the cold

The Arctic and the Antarctic are the coldest places on Earth. This is because, during the winter, they get hardly any sun (see pages 2–3). Also, any rays that do shine are reflected back into space by the polar ice caps, which act like giant mirrors.

Water can turn from boiling to freezing in less than a second.

Spilled ice
When it's this cold outside (-60°F/-51°C), a cup of boiling water thrown into the air turns to ice crystals before it hits the ground.

Off the scale
In the winter, the average Antarctic temperature is -76°F (-60°C). The coldest place on Earth is Vostok, well inland, where a record low of -128°F (-89°C) has been recorded.

10

Blinding light

Extreme polar landscapes are bleak, with no trees, people, or buildings in sight. Here, snow glitters in the sunshine and produces a glare so bright it can hurt your eyes. This is called snow blindness.

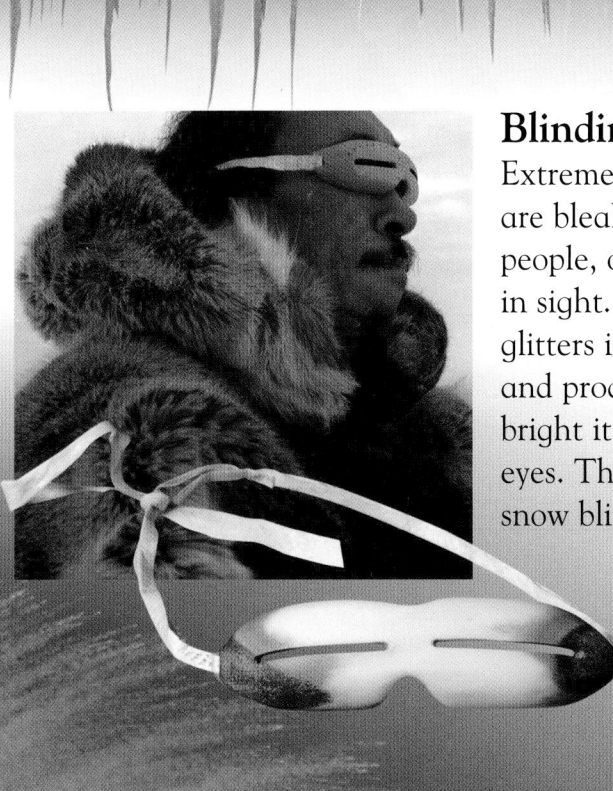

Native people make sun goggles out of reindeer antler or skin.

Frost damage

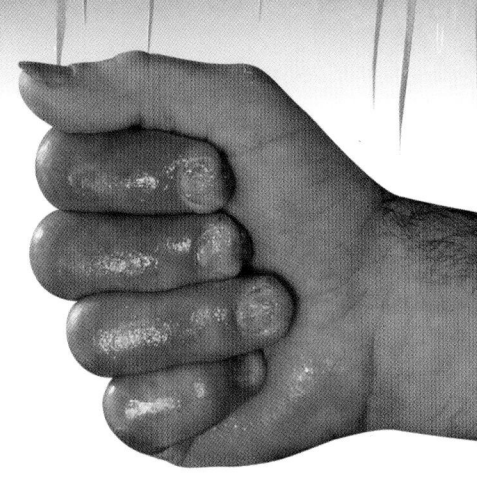

Frostbite happens when flesh freezes and dies. If only surface layers are frozen, the skin peels off like a sunburn. But if large areas freeze, then feet, hands, fingers, or toes may have to be removed—or they fall off!

Cold cover

Animal skin and fur make the warmest clothes. If they're sewn with muscle fiber, which swells when it's wet, the seams are waterproof too.

Heads and faces need to be warmly wrapped.

AND THEN THERE WERE NONE

American adventurer Robert Peary completed his 1909 trek to the North Pole (see pages 38-39) without losing any of his toes to frostbite. This is because he had no toes left— they had all dropped off on previous polar adventures!

Polar lights

In both polar landscapes, you can see fantastical light shows in the night sky. These are called aurora borealis, or northern lights, in the Arctic, and aurora australis, or southern lights, in the Antarctic.

"Aurora" is the Latin word for dawn.

Some people think the lights make soft sounds.

Curve with rays

Here an arc, or curve, of light crosses the sky from east to west. It breaks up into long and short rays that dance up and down.

Crown

When the colored light shimmers out in a fan from the center, the shape is called a corona. The word corona is Latin for "crown."

Red lights over Alaska

What do they look like?

Sometimes auroras are dazzling and bright, and sometimes they're so faint you can hardly see them. Either way, they appear in many different shapes or "formations."

Smooth band

Still stripes of smooth, colored light across the sky are called homogenous (say ha-maw-jen-us) bands. This word means "the same all through."

Curtain

These lights fill the sky with wide bands of wavy light that change all the time from bright to dim and back again.

Light colors

Auroras are formed when energy particles from the Sun hit gases in the air. Different gases produce different colors of light.

Oxygen

Oxygen with hydrogen

Nitrogen

Big bear

Polar bears are the biggest bears in the world. They look cute and cuddly, but they are fierce hunters who can kill anything—human or animal—that gets too near.

Magnified many times, each hair looks like this.

Bear hair

Polar bears' hairs are hollow—like thick white tubes. The air inside helps to keep out the cold and stops their fur from matting.

A bigger splash

Polar bears are natural swimmers. They can stay in freezing water for a long time, paddling with their huge front paws.

Seal meal

Hungry polar bears love a tasty seal or walrus supper on the ice. When they make a kill, they eat the skin and blubber first. If they're not very hungry, most of the meat gets left for another bear, or for passing birds that like to feed on dead animals.

Females sometimes give birth to one cub, or three, but they usually have two.

Heating pad

In addition to fur, polar bears have a thick layer of fat called blubber. Here, twin cubs snuggle up to their mother's warm, soft, squishy body.

Moms look after their babies for two or three years.

Footprints in the frost

Polar bears' big furry paws have bumpy soles that help them walk on snow and ice without sinking or slipping around.

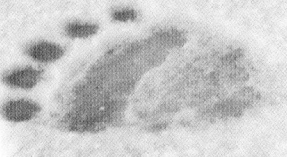

Man—polar bears' only enemy—can use their tracks to hunt them.

Black and white

While a polar bear's head, its body, and even its feet, are covered with thick, creamy-white hairs; its skin, nose, mouth, and tongue are black. Long sharp teeth allow it to tear the flesh off the prey it kills.

Penguin parade

Why aren't penguins afraid of polar bears? Because penguins make their home in the Antarctic, where there are no polar bears. Only two species, Emperor and Adélie, live in Antarctica itself, but several other varieties are found in the surrounding seas.

Safety in numbers
Antarctic penguins live in large colonies on the sea ice. Emperors, the largest variety, don't build nests, but keep their babies (called chicks) warm next to their bodies.

I'm hungry!
Penguins recognize and respond to each other's cries, which is just as well, since this Emperor baby is shouting for his supper. Both Mom and Dad store food in their stomachs, then bring it up again to feed their young.

Penguin facts

- Penguins drink both fresh- and saltwater.

- Emperors can stay under water for up to 20 minutes.

- When penguins catch fish, they swallow them whole.

- Adult Emperors are as tall as a 3- or 4-year-old child.

Water wings

Penguins eat fish and seafood. To catch it, these Emperors can dive far below the ocean's surface. They glide through the water as if they're flying, but the closest they come to real flying is when they leap out again—and belly flop on the ice!

Making a home

The smaller Adélie penguins build nests on rocky coasts and islands. The nests are made from small stones carried in the birds' beaks and dropped into place.

Smile for the camera!

Other varieties of penguin, including Gentoo, Macaroni, King, Chinstrap, and Humbolt, live nearby. This one's goofy "smile" is actually a line of black feathers under his beak. Can you guess what kind he is?　(Chinstrap)

17

Happy wanderer

The wandering albatross breeds in the Antarctic, then flies off for weeks at a time to look for food. With its 10 ft (3 m) wingspan, it can cover 550 miles (885 km) in a day.

Birds that fly

Although penguins are birds, they can't fly. Some flying birds live only in the Arctic, and some live in the Antarctic, but there is one bird that flies from one place to the other every year!

Partners for life

Black-browed albatrosses never stray far from the places they were born. When they mate, they stay with the same partner for life, raising one chick a year in a sturdy nest made from mud and grass.

Feathery meal

During the summer, south polar skuas feed on Adélie penguin eggs, and sometimes on the baby penguins. For convenience, they build their nests near Adélie colonies.

Flying facts

- A champion flyer, the wandering albatross can reach speeds of 50 mph (80 kph).

- Albatrosses can spend weeks in the air without landing.

- The wandering albatross has the longest wing span of any living bird.

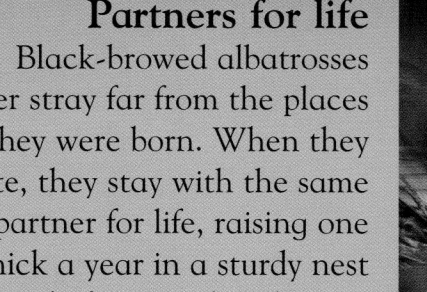

Tiny traveler

Hovering low over Arctic seas, chubby little auks (slightly smaller than doves) dive for food and use their wings to "fly" under water. Little auks breed in huge colonies in rocky crevices.

Tern and tern about

Arctic terns breed in the north, but fly to the Antarctic every year. They usually live for about 20 years—enough time for them to travel almost 400,000 miles (645,000 km)!

White hunter

Male snowy owls have pure white feathers so they can hunt in the snow without being spotted. Their favorite snack is a small lemming.

Snow hooves

Some large mammals manage in the Arctic because their feet, or hooves, can grip the ice and snow. These animals include caribou, reindeer (their smaller, tamer cousins), and horned, hairy musk oxen.

Hooves are made for walking

Both reindeer and caribou have three toes that spread out when they're walking to act like big, flat snow shoes.

On the move

The Sami people of northern Lapland keep reindeer in large herds. Every spring, they all move north to the coast, where the reindeer have their babies.

Both male and female caribou (and reindeer) have antlers.

Reindeer skin makes warm, furry boots for the Sami people.

Arctic ruler

There are more caribou in the Arctic than any other large mammal. The Inuit (pp. 34) use their meat for food and their skin for clothes. Long ago, they made tents from it as well, and burned caribou fat as fuel.

This thick, coarse hair is so long that it hangs to the ground like a skirt.

Sharp horns help musk oxen to defend themselves and to attack if they're threatened.

On their own

Although they belong to the same family as cows, sheep, and goats, musk oxen don't look like any other creature. They are short—about 5 ft (1.5 m)—but very heavy.

Cozy covering

Musk oxen are the only Arctic mammals who never look for shelter, no matter how cold and snowy it gets. Their winter coats are thick enough to keep them toasty warm.

If they're attacked, musk oxen form a safe circle.

Males are on the outside, with females and babies inside.

Head to head

Male musk oxen perform a kind of duel called "jousting." They walk away from each other, then turn and charge, crashing horns. This is repeated over and over until one of them gives up.

CHRISTMAS CREATURES

The image of Santa Claus in a reindeer-driven sleigh first appeared in the 1822 poem *A Visit from St. Nicholas* ("'Twas the Night Before Christmas ..."). In 1939, more than 100 years later, the American department store Montgomery Ward published a 20th-century update— *Rudolph the Red Nosed Reindeer,* written by one of its employees as a Christmas giveaway book.

Small furry animals

When you think of Arctic animals, you probably imagine giant polar bears and herds of reindeer and caribou. But lots of smaller mammals live in the far north too.

Lemmings are small, round, and plump.

Sleepy-time squirrel

Known to the Inuit as "siksiks," Arctic ground squirrels hibernate (go into a deep sleep) all winter. Large groups of them live together in underground burrows.

Somebody's supper?

This Siberian lemming copes with the snow by digging under it, where he nibbles plant roots. If he comes out, he may get eaten by a snowy owl.

When I wake up, I want my dinner!

Snarling stalker

Wolverines are small, fierce creatures with huge appetites. They often hunt much bigger animals like caribou and moose, as well as lemmings, voles, squirrels, and birds.

Seasonal shades

Arctic foxes come in two winter colors—white and "blue," which is actually gray/blue. In summer, they are brownish on their backs and heads, and cream-colored on their tummies.

"Blue" Arctic fox

White Arctic fox

Some Arctic hares have snow-white fur with black ear-tips.

My hairs are hollow, like a polar bear's.

Luxury coat

Arctic hares are the biggest of all the hares, and the only ones that live in the Arctic. They have soft, thick, silky coats.

Black-tipped ermine tails circle the base of this jeweled crown.

Howling hunters

Arctic wolves come from the same family as gray or timber wolves. They are nearly always light in color—white, off-white, cream, or pale gray—so they don't stand out against the snow.

Royal fur

A kind of small weasel, ermines are brown in summer and pure white in winter. Their precious fur often decorates royal regalia.

Walking on fins

Seals and walruses belong to the group of mammals known as *"pinnipeds"* (meaning fin feet). They have flippers instead of feet, and streamlined bodies that move easily through water.

Thick skinned

Walrus skin is very thick—up to 1½ in (4 cm)—with deep creases to provide protection and insulation. Walruses live in the Arctic—there are none in Antarctica.

Male walruses can grow up to 11 ft (3.5 m)

Breathing holes

Seals breathe through holes in the surface ice. They dig these out with their teeth and their toenails.

Adult walruses have big tusks, which they use mostly to frighten their enemies.

Weddell seals eat shrimp, octopus, and fish. To find food, they stay under water for up to 45 minutes.

Crabeater seal

When he's not busy breathing, this Antarctic crabeater seal snacks on tiny krill (see pages 30-31), which he filters out of the water through his teeth.

Southern swimmers

Weddell seals thrive in seas that are just 800 miles (1,290 km) from the South Pole. These creatures live farther south than any other mammal on Earth.

Turning pink

Male walruses (called bulls) lie close together in the summer sun. When their hair falls out, it reveals dark pink skin underneath.

and weigh up to 3,750 lbs (1,700 kg).

Fat and hairy

Walruses are huge and awkward on land, and very very fat— their blubber can be more than 4 in (10 cm) thick. On the outside is a thin layer of hair that falls out in the summer.

Harp seals live in deep water among floating Arctic ice floes.

Flipper facts

● Southern elephant seals were nearly wiped out by hunters wanting their skins and oils.

● Walruses prefer seas that are less than 260 ft (80 m) deep.

● Only the Antarctic leopard seal eats other seals.

● Walruses spend two-thirds of their lives in water.

Baby harps

Harp seals, who live in the Arctic, produce babies (pups) in late winter. Some of these pups, called whitecoats, are killed for their fur.

Sea giants

Whales are huge sea mammals. Some have sharp teeth to catch prey, but others get food by filtering vast amounts of water through huge, tough fringes dangling inside their mouth. These fringes are called baleen.

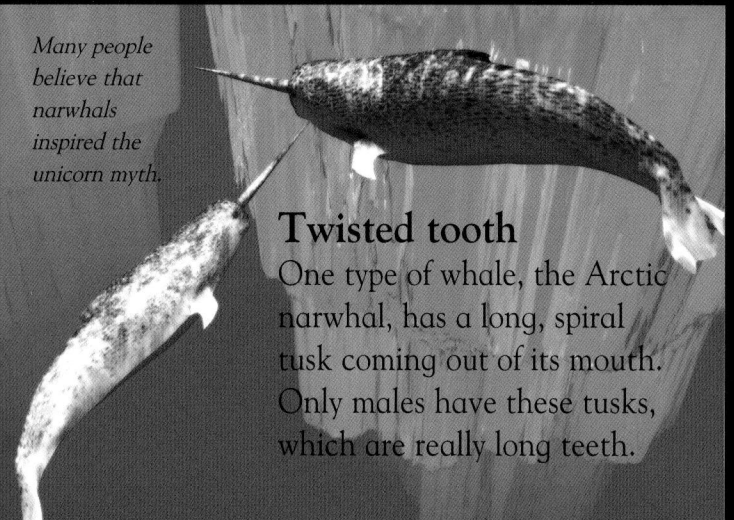

Many people believe that narwhals inspired the unicorn myth.

Twisted tooth

One type of whale, the Arctic narwhal, has a long, spiral tusk coming out of its mouth. Only males have these tusks, which are really long teeth.

Mini monsters

Compared to other whales, minkes are small. Antarctic minkes—around 33 ft (10 m) long—are baleen whales that spend their summers swimming in pack ice. A group of Adélie penguins are keeping a close eye on this one!

Let's see a smile!

Small like narwhals, adult beluga whales are white, with what looks like smiling faces. They have teeth, not tusks, and eat Arctic fish and seafood.

Off with the old!

Belugas are sociable, and travel in big groups called *gams*. Once a year, they roll around together in gravelly shallow water to scrape off their old skin and reveal new skin underneath.

Cruel cargo

In the past, thousands of Arctic bowhead whales were killed for their baleen, which was used to make combs, brushes, umbrellas, and corsets! Only a few of them are hunted now, but they are still a rare and endangered species.

Fine food

Tiny creatures like these (magnified hundreds of times in this picture) are filtered out from the huge quantities of water baleen whales take in.

SMALL CATCH

Minke whales got their name from a greedy 18th-century whale fisherman (or "whaler"). Even hundreds of years ago, there were rules against catching small whales, but Minke caught them anyway. Eventually, other whalers began to call small whales "Minke's whales," and the name stuck.

27

Southern seas

The oceans around Antarctica are freezing cold and partly covered with winter ice. Divers brave enough to explore this hidden world will discover a surprising collection

Magic fluid

Twisting its way through the dark water, this amazing icefish has see-through blood that acts like antifreeze—it stays liquid even at freezing temperatures.

Jellyfish drift along with the ocean current.

Pink jelly

This Antarctic jellyfish, which lives near the surface, has a frilly bell that's more than three feet (1 meter) wide.

Southern sea facts

- Tiny plants called algae live underneath pack ice, so it sometimes looks pale green.

- Even in winter, the water hovers near the freezing point, so it's warmer than the land.

- In addition to the creatures shown, sponges, crabs, and sea anemones live in this icy sea.

Winter visitors

To find the fantastic creatures living in ice caves under the Weddell Sea, divers drop in through seals' breathing holes.

Share and share alike

This golden sea star cuddles up to a featherduster worm—he may want to share the food particles on its gills. Like many creatures who live here, sea stars gather under breathing holes because they feed on seal droppings.

Sea food

In addition to providing food for birds, mammals, and other fish, both polar oceans contain many kinds of fish and seafood that people like to eat.

Some holes are made with a chisel or a pick, while others are drilled.

Supper from the sea
The Inuit people eat lots of fish, which they sometimes catch through holes in the Arctic ice.

Braving the ice
Making their way through floating polar ice, these bright red fishing boats operate out of West Greenland.

Frozen meals
Polar cod live in ice-covered Arctic waters, feeding on algae underneath the ice. Native peoples eat them, and birds and bigger fish eat them too, but they are not caught and sold by commercial fisheries.

Polar cod have slightly jutting bottom jaws so they can scrape algae from underneath the ice.

Fish are tied on racks to dry quickly in the open air.

Winter supplies

Even in the cool Arctic, fish don't stay fresh for long. When there are plenty available in the summer, native peoples dry some of them to provide food for the winter months.

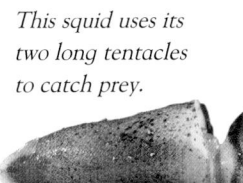

This squid uses its two long tentacles to catch prey.

Quick return

Lots of sea creatures eat Antarctic squid, and commercial fisheries are beginning to take an interest too. There are so many squid, and they grow so fast, that some people call them "weeds of the sea."

Antarctic krill have clear shells and big black eyes.

Cash catch

Pink salmon in the Arctic Ocean return to freshwater in big groups to breed, which they do only once. They are so important to the fishing industry that they are often called "bread-and-butter fish."

In for the krill

Bright pink krill feed on tiny plants in the seas around Antarctica. They are eaten by seals, penguins, whales, sea birds, and, in Japan and eastern Europe, people.

Brave blooms

The Antarctic is so cold that hardly any plants can live there. But temperatures are warmer in some Arctic areas, so a few hardy flowers and leaves make a bright summer show.

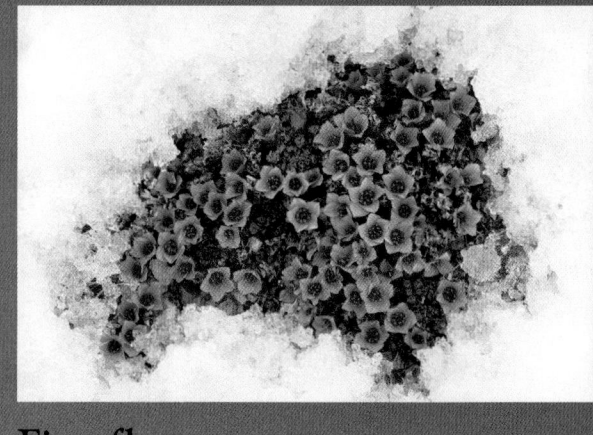

First flower
Pretty purple saxifrage is one of the first plants to flower in the Arctic spring. It has lots of showy cup-shaped blossoms on short, leafy stems.

Creepy spider
The long red "legs" on this spider plant—called *stolons*—stretch out and grow new plants at each tip.

Sunny face
To catch as many rays as possible, the Arctic poppy tries to turn its cheerful yellow face toward the Sun. In a few places, Arctic poppies are white.

Cozy coat

The mastadon flower's hairy stem and leaves help protect it from the cold. One clue to this plant's family (it's a kind of sunflower) is the round cluster of golden blooms on top.

Drop-in dinner

The reindeer droppings that have landed right on top of this alpine saxifrage will provide it with lots of nourishing food.

Arctic poppies like cool places best.

In their own language, the word Inuit means "the people."

Arctic peoples

Antarctica is so cold and so dry that only a few scientists live there. At the other end of the Earth, though, the far northern regions of Canada, Europe, and Russia are home to lots of native peoples.

Inuit
In northern Canada, modern Inuit people live in ordinary houses. Some hunters, when they travel long distances, build traditional snow shelters called igloos.

About four million people live in the Arctic.

CANADA

GREENLAND

Sami
The Sami people in northern Norway travel long distances with their reindeer. This female herder uses a large antler to help her move the animals around.

Traditional Sami dress is red and blue, with fancy woven belts and ribbon trim.

Chukchi

The Chukchi live in eastern Siberia, so the Inuit are their neighbors. Both peoples use wooden boats covered in walrus skin to hunt sea mammals.

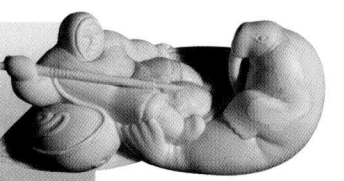

Chukchi carvers use walrus ivory to record their traditions. Here, a hunter spears his prey.

Dolgan

The Dolgan people travel around Siberia's Taymyr Peninsula, living in portable huts called baloks. These are built on runners so they can be pulled by reindeer.

RUSSIAN FEDERATION

ARCTIC

Clothes made from reindeer fur keep this little Dolgan boy cozy and warm.

Also dressed in reindeer fur, this Nenets woman feeds boiled fish to two pet reindeer.

LAPLAND

Nenets

There have been Nenets people in northern Siberia for over 1,000 years. Like the Sami, they keep reindeer to provide them with food, clothing, shelter, and transportation.

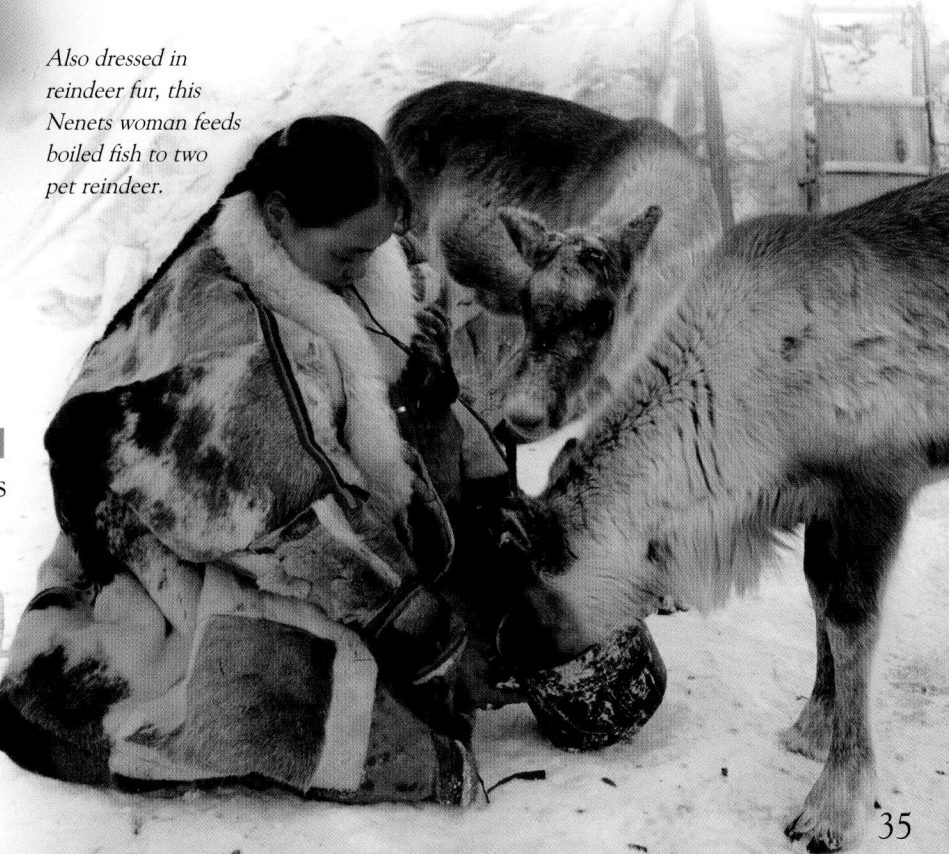

The modern world

Polar lands are not just vast landscapes of ice and snow—there are lots of modern towns in the Arctic. Antarctica has no towns, but there are important scientific research centers there.

This balloon will gather information about the Earth's ozone layer.

Working for the world

Antarctic research stations provide important scientific information on lots of subjects, including climate, weather, wildlife, pollution, and space.

The Amundsen-Scott station

Look out above!

The McMurdo station is Antarctica's largest community. Here, two scientists based there send up balloons that will help them to learn about the Earth's atmosphere.

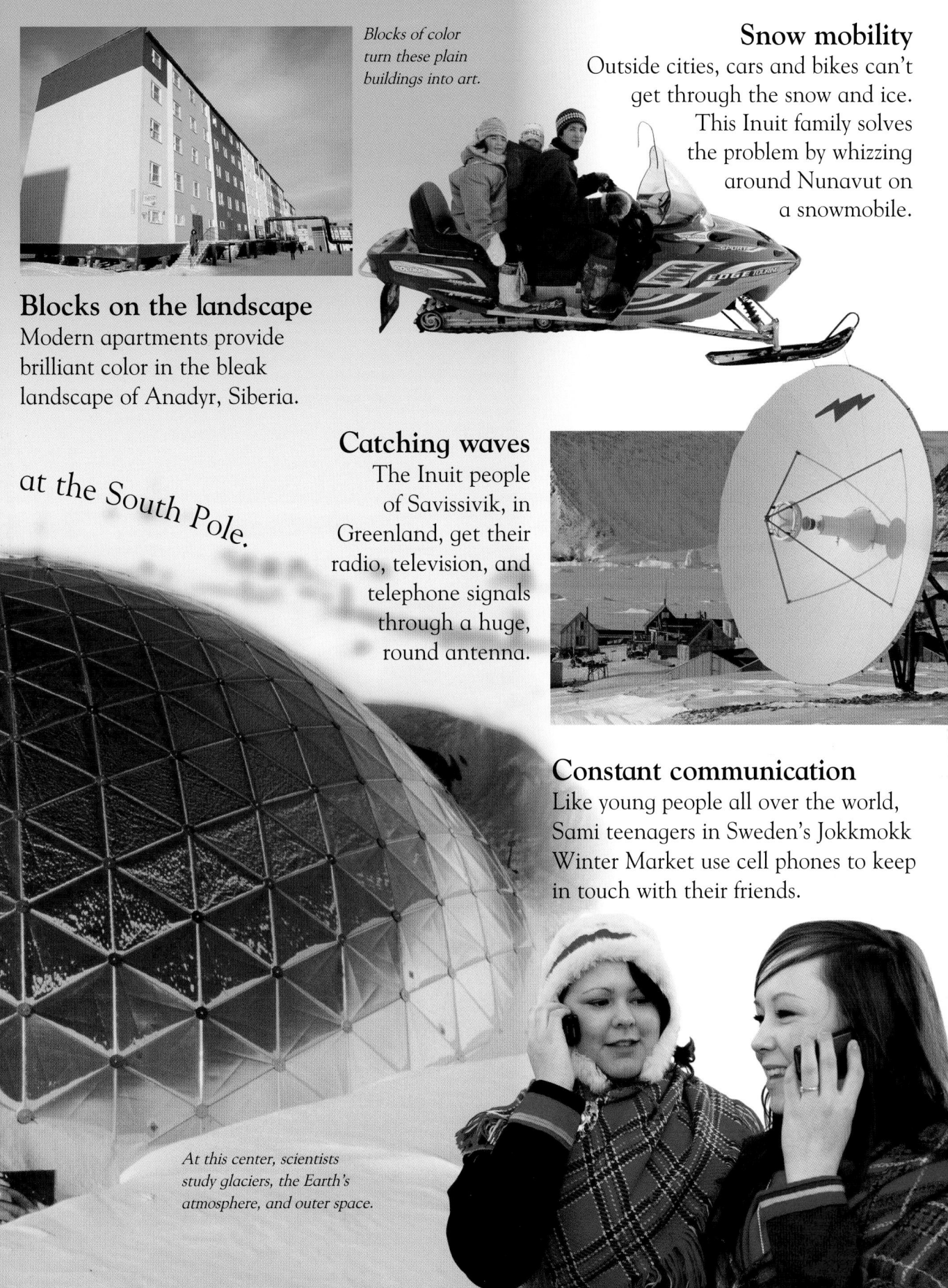

Blocks of color turn these plain buildings into art.

Snow mobility

Outside cities, cars and bikes can't get through the snow and ice. This Inuit family solves the problem by whizzing around Nunavut on a snowmobile.

Blocks on the landscape

Modern apartments provide brilliant color in the bleak landscape of Anadyr, Siberia.

at the South Pole.

Catching waves

The Inuit people of Savissivik, in Greenland, get their radio, television, and telephone signals through a huge, round antenna.

Constant communication

Like young people all over the world, Sami teenagers in Sweden's Jokkmokk Winter Market use cell phones to keep in touch with their friends.

At this center, scientists study glaciers, the Earth's atmosphere, and outer space.

Poles or bust

For nearly 200 years, daring adventurers have set out to reach the poles. Some of them came back to tell their stories, while others met their death in the icy wasteland.

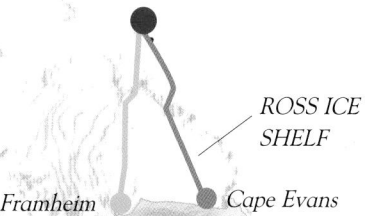

Amundsen's route ————
Scott's route ————

ANTARCTICA

SOUTH POLE

ROSS ICE SHELF

Framheim   *Cape Evans*

Scott's Terra Nova was once a Scottish whaling ship.

Race to the bottom

In 1911, two expeditions sailed off from their own lands to race to the South Pole: a British team led by Robert Scott, and a Norwegian party led by Roald Amundsen.

Team Britain

Robert Scott made a few mistakes in planning, and his team hit freakishly cold and dangerous weather. They were beaten by the Norwegians, and they all died on the journey home.

Expedition facts

- When Scott arrived at the South Pole, he wrote in his diary, "This is an awful place."

- In 1879, a small US ship, the *Jeanette*, set off for the North Pole, but got crushed by ice.

- Antarctica was only discovered in the early 1800s.

Amundsen's ship Fram in front of Scott's Terra Nova, Antarctica, 1911.

Win for Norway

The Norwegians took plenty of supplies and traveled by skis and dogsleds. They reached the pole five weeks before Scott and left a flag and a tent there for him to find.

Double triumph

Fifteen years later, in 1926, Roald Amundsen (above) arrived at the North Pole by balloon. He was the first person in history to travel to both poles.

Peary's route `------`

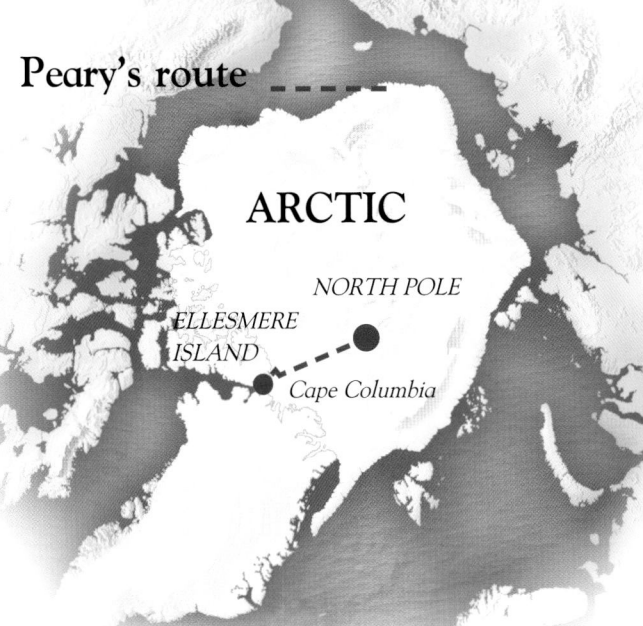

ARCTIC

NORTH POLE

ELLESMERE ISLAND

Cape Columbia

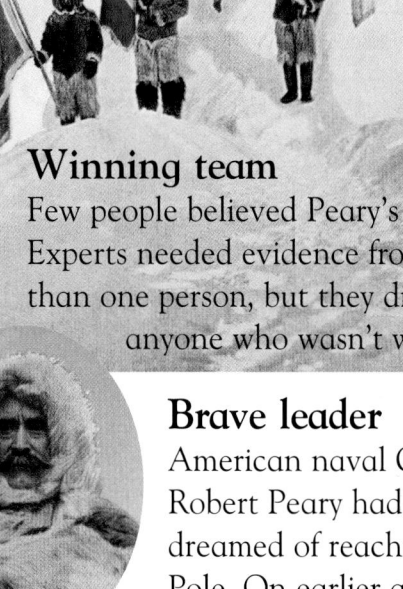

Winning team
Few people believed Peary's claims. Experts needed evidence from more than one person, but they didn't trust anyone who wasn't white.

Reaching the top
Robert Peary, Matthew Henson (an African American), and a mostly Inuit team started off for the North Pole from Cape Columbia in 1909. A few were sent back on the way, but those who arrived claimed an incredibly fast time of 37 days.

Brave leader
American naval Commander Robert Peary had always dreamed of reaching the North Pole. On earlier attempts, he lost his toes to frostbite!

We know it can be done!

Avery's crew recreate the historic image of Peary's team, above.

Modern hero
In 2005, British explorer Tom Avery set out with the same kinds of dogs and sleds as Peary. Avery duplicated Peary's journey and matched his time.

No way back
Global warming causes the Arctic ice to melt earlier and earlier each year, so Avery could not follow Peary's return trail.

Faithful friends
Like Peary, Avery (right) used eight Canadian Inuit dogs to pull each sled. These are much stronger than regular huskies.

Animal power

In freezing temperatures and dangerous conditions, animals often provide the best form of transportation. Breeding and training them to pull heavy loads is an important part of many Arctic cultures.

Winning team

In heavy snow and ice, most normal loads are pulled by teams of husky dogs, who offer the perfect combination of strength, speed, and resistance to cold.

Follow the leader

Each dog has its own position on a sled team. The lead dog is always harnessed first, and released last, because the others get upset if they're attached to the sled without a leader at the front.

Reindeer removals

Dolgan reindeer herders in Siberia take their huts—called baloks—with them on their travels. To do this, they build the huts on runners, then hitch them to a team of reindeer.

The Inuit have been breeding huskies for over a thousand years.

Racing with reindeer

As well as using reindeer for transportation, the Sami people race them in competitions. This one involves small sleds, single reindeer, and racers on their bellies!

Dogs that work

Most working dogs in the Arctic are either huskies, malamutes (who are slower, but can carry heavier loads), or samoyeds (Siberian dogs that herd reindeer *and* pull small sleds).

Samoyed   *Malamute*   *Husky*

41

Underground treasure

In both the Arctic and the Antarctic, rich natural resources lie buried under ground. The terms of the Antarctic Treaty won't let anyone touch what's there, but Arctic oil, coal, gas, and minerals bring money and jobs to the countries that own them.

This huge oil pipeline

ARCTIC OCEAN

Prudhoe Bay

ALASKA (USA)

Valdez

PACIFIC OCEAN

Costly fuel
It took 21,000 workers to build the Alaska Pipeline, which carries oil to Valdez, an ice-free port in the south. During construction, 31 workers died in accidents.

Copper ore

Gold

Platinum

Iron ore

Metal mining
Lots of different minerals lie buried in the Arctic, including iron, tin, copper, zinc, coal, platinum, uranium, and nickel. This backhoe loads nickel ore near Norilsk, Siberia.

Russian resources

Siberia in Russia contains one of the largest deposits of natural gas in the world. This rig is drilling gas from the ground near Bovanenkovo on the Yamal Peninsula.

Gas

"0" indicates the pipeline's starting point.

Crude oil

Coal

Plants on fire

Coal, oil, and gas are all fossil fuels, which means that, millions of years ago, they were formed from dead plants that didn't rot away completely.

goes on and on for 795 miles (1,270 km) across Alaska.

Underground facts

● The Alaska Pipeline is regularly checked by PIGs— Pipeline Inspection Gauges.

● As well as fuels and industrial minerals, Arctic mines produce gold and diamonds.

● Siberian oil contributes lots and lots of money to the Russian economy.

43

World in peril

It's easy to damage our Earth—even the far ends of it! In the Arctic, mining and oil-drilling harm animals and landscapes. While Antarctica is protected from industry, even visiting tourists can hurt its environment.

Environment facts

- When the ozone layer is damaged, strong sun can cause bad sunburn and skin cancers.

- Chemicals and mining waste dumped into Arctic rivers pollute the ocean too.

- If all the Antarctic ice melted, the oceans would rise by 200 feet (60 meters).

Industrial waste
Discarded oil drums rust away very slowly in the cold, dry Arctic air. On the Melville Peninsula in northern Canada, garbage like this spoils the landscape and threatens wildlife.

Oil spill
Sometimes oil pipes crack, or tankers—huge ships that carry oil—break up in the sea. When this happens, thick black sludge leaks out and poisons the landscape. This oil-polluted lake is in western Siberia.

Ozone hole

Very low ozone level

Low ozone level

Average ozone level

Ozone depletion
Wrapped around the Earth is a layer of invisible gas called ozone, which helps block damaging rays from the Sun. Pollution has made holes in the ozone layer at both poles.

Antarctica viewed from space

Warming up
Burning fossil fuels create a kind of pollution that makes the Earth warmer. When the poles warm up, the ice, like this Arctic slab, starts to melt.

Tourists are asked not to leave waste behind, or interfere with wildlife in any way.

Polar sightseeing
Travel companies arrange special cruises for people who want to visit Antarctica. Here, tourists explore Paradise Harbor from inflatable rubber rafts.

Glossary

Here are the meanings of some words that are useful when you're learning about the Arctic and the Antarctic.

algae tiny plants that live in water and provide food for fish and marine mammals.

atmosphere the wide band of air above our Earth.

aurora australis the bands of colored light that appear in the sky over Antarctica.

aurora borealis the bands of colored light that appear in the sky over the Arctic.

baleen brushlike fringe that some whales have at the back of their mouth to strain food from the water.

balok portable hut on runners used by the traveling Dolgan people of Siberia. Baloks are pulled by reindeer.

blubber the thick layer of fat that protects some animals (like whales and seals) from the cold.

breed to produce babies.

burrow a hole in the ground that animals live in. Ground squirrels have burrows.

colony a group of animals (such as penguins) that live together.

environment the natural world all around us, including land, air, and living things.

expedition a trip people take for a particular purpose, such as exploration.

freezing what happens when water turns into solid ice.

frost ice crystals that form when moisture in the air freezes.

frostbite the damage caused when parts of a living creature (like fingers or toes) freeze.

gam a large group of whales that all travel together.

gas a light, invisible, airlike substance that has no shape of its own.

glacier a slow-moving mass of ice formed from the snow that falls on mountains and ice caps.

hemisphere half a ball shape. Our Earth has two hemispheres: northern and southern.

herd a large group of animals that travel together.

hibernate to go into a long, deep sleep, usually during the winter. Many bears and squirrels hibernate.

hooves the curved, horny feet on some animals like horses and reindeer.

ice water that gets so cold it freezes solid.

iceberg a large chunk of ice that breaks off a glacier or an ice cap and floats away in the sea.

ice cap a very large mass of ice that is made from built-up snow that never melts.

ice crystals tiny pieces of ice formed from hundreds of straight-sided particles.

ice floe a chunk or sheet of floating sea ice.

insulation material used to keep warmth or cold (or even sound) in one place.

ivory the name given to tusks or horns when they're polished and turned into jewelry or objects.

mammal a warm-blooded animal that drinks its mother's milk when it's a baby.

native used about people, animals, and plants to mean that they belong in a particular place. The Inuit are native to the Arctic.

pack ice the large masses of ice that result when frozen sea ice breaks up.

pancake ice the rounded chunks of ice that are formed when small floes knock into each other so their edges become rounded.

plankton the mass of tiny plants and animals that float around in the sea and provide food for marine animals.

polar connected to either the North Pole or the South Pole.

pollution anything that makes air, earth, snow, ice, or water dirty or poisonous.

snow clusters of ice crystals that freeze directly from the air, without turning into drops of water first. Ice crystals stick together to form snowflakes before they fall.

tusk a hard, toothlike horn. Some walruses have long tusks.

tentacle a long, flexible armlike body part that water creatures like squid and octopus use for touching and grasping.

wing span the distance from the tip of one wing to the tip of the other when the wings are outstretched.

Index

Polar bear

Acknowledgments

Dorling Kindersley would like to thank:
Andy Cooke for his original illustrations; Peter Bull for maps; Martin Copeland and Rose Horridge for picture research administration; and Zahavit Shalev and Carrie Love for editorial assistance.

Picture credits

The publisher would like to thank the following for their kind permission to reproduce their photographs:
a=above; c=center; b=below; l=left; r=right; t=top;

Alamy Images: Bryan & Cherry Alexander Photography 30tl, 30cr, 30bl; Steve Bloom Images 18tc; Eureka 23bl; Leslie Garland Picture Library 6tl; Popperfoto 38cl. **Bryan and Cherry Alexander Photography:** 4bl, 6-7 (Background), 7cla, 7cra, 7cl, 7cr, 8bl, 9cr, 10t, 10-11b, 11t, 11cl, 11br, 15tr, 15c, 16-17, 17cb, 19 (Background), 20tr, 20cl, 24cl, 32tr, 32cl, 33tr, 33cl, 34t, 34b, 35tl, 35tr, 35cr, 35br, 37tl, 37tr, 37cr, 37br, 40-41, 41t, 42br, 42-43, 43tc, 44-45, 45tl, 45cr, 48 (Background); Paul Drummond 24bl; Ann Hawthorne 6bl, 36cl, 36-37; Hans Jensen 32-33; David Rootes 24crb, 31bc, 31br; Mark Ryan 16l; Frank

Todd 5br, 19bl, 26cra. **Tom Avery:** 39clb, 39bc. **Barclays Capital North:** Tom Avery 39br. **British Antarctic Survey:** 31cra. **Corbis:** 38bl; Bettmann 38cb, 39tr; Ralph A. Clevenger 8-9; W. Perry Conway 18l; Daniel J. Cox 13tl; Tim Davis 1; Hulton-Deutsch Collection 38c; Jacques Langevin 21c; Chris Rainier 7br; D. Robert & Lorri Franz 22br; Galen Rowell 5tl; Setboun 41cr; Joseph Sohm/Visions of America 45br; Stapleton Collection 39c; Winfred Wisniewski/ Frank Lane Picture Agency 46-47. **Daryl Pederson/D&M Photo Inc:** 12tr. **DK Images:** Colin Keates/Natural History Museum, London 42fclb, 42fclb (gold); Harry Taylor/Natural History Museum, London 42clb. **FLPA - images of nature:** Michael Quinton/Minden Pictures 31cl; Roger Tidman 31t; Winfried Wisniewski 18br; Norbert Wu/Minden Pictures 17cra, 28bl, 28-29, 29tr. **Getty Images:** Hulton Archive 11cla; The Image Bank 41br; Science Faction 12-13, 13tr; Stock Image 23fbl; Stone 12tl, 19br, 20-21; Visuals Unlimited 11cra. **ImageState/Pictor:** Mark Newman 17br. **N.H.P.A:** Hellio & Van Ingen 22cra; Alan Williams 19tl; OSF/photolibrary.com: Daniel Cox 3r. **Science Photo Library:** Doug Allan 26crb; Christian Darkin 26cl; Bernhard Edmaier 5tr; Richard Ellis 27t; NASA 45c; Mark Newman 14bl; Andrew Syred 14cl, 27cb. **Seapics.com:** 15crb, 21tc, 21br; Michael S. Nolan 23cla. **Still Pictures:** Kelvin Aitken 24-25; Carlo Dani & Ingrid Jeske 25br; Patrick Frischknecht 25tr; Steven Kazlowski 14-15, 22l; Lynn Rogers 15bl; Kevin Schafer 26bl; Norbert Wu 28c. **Zefa Visual Media:** A & S Carey 23br.

All other images © Dorling Kindersley

For further information see: www.dkimages.com